Always tell the truth

This book belongs to

_____

Written by Stephen Barnett
Illustrated by Rosie Brooks

Contents

About this book

The book inspires children to be helpful, honest and generous. Questions at the end test the child's attention and the new words section encourage vocabulary building.

Help others, and others will help you

There was football practice after
school that day. I
hurried home to pick up my
shoes and then go for practice.

On reaching home my father
said that first I had to feed the
dog and the fish.

I thought I would be late for football practice and miss out on all the fun too!

Just then, my older sister Sally
came from school. When
she saw me in a hurry, she
offered to help.

What a kind sister! She looked
after Jimmy, our dog, while I
gave food to the fish.

Later that night when we were doing our homework, Sally's pen broke. And she did not have another pen.

I told her that I had a spare pen
which she could keep.

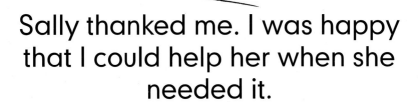

Sally thanked me. I was happy that I could help her when she needed it.

The next day, my father said that
if you are helpful to others, others
will be helpful to you too.

Always tell the truth

I was playing with my ball. I
didn't look where I was going
and I ran over my mother's
flowers.

I tried to stand them up. But some
of their stems were broken!
I hoped mother would not see
them.

I thought, maybe I should tell my mother at once about breaking the stems of the flowers.

Later my mother called me and
asked me what had happened
to her flowers.

Oh! I was worried that if I told her
the truth, my mother would be
angry with me.

But I had been taught to tell
the truth. So I told her what had
happened. I said sorry too!

My mother was quiet for a
moment. Then she praised me for
telling the truth.

It is better to share

Lily and I were walking home from school. Suddenly, we saw a tree with a ripe peach hanging from it

Lily wanted the peach as she
thought that she had seen it first.

I wanted it too as I thought I had
seen it first.

Lily and I pushed each other
and tried to grab the peach. We
shouted at each other too!

We shook the branch and
the peach fell off the tree. It
crashed to the ground and was
squashed!

No one could eat it. We walked
home very quietly. We were
upset.

On reaching home, we told my
father what had happened.

Father said that we should not have been greedy. If we had shared the peach, we could have both eaten it.

We promised to share next time.
Then my father shared some
sweets with us.

New words

football	stems	wanted
practice	broken	peach
hurried	hoped	pushed
reaching	breaking	grab
feed	happened	shouted
brush	worried	shook
thought	truth	crashed
offered	angry	squashed
help	taught	quickly
kind	sorry	walked
homework	moment	reaching
broke	praised	happened
spare	walking	shared
thanked	ripe	promised
helpful	hanging	next
playing	suddenly	sweets
tried	saw	

What did you learn?

Help others, and others will help you
How did Sally help her brother?
What is the name of their dog?

Always tell the truth
What colour are the flowers in the garden?
How were the flowers broken?
Did the child tell the truth?

It is better to share
Where were the children walking to?
Which fruit was hanging from a tree?
What did the children learn in this story?